HEART MECHANIC

Poems by Gisela Ruebsaat

Quadra Books

Library and Archives Canada Cataloguing in Publication

Ruebsaat, Gisela, author
        Heart mechanic : poems / Gisela Renate Ruebsaat.

ISBN 978-0-9939223-4-3 (paperback)

        I. Title.

PS8635.U375H43 2016   C811'.6   C2016-903597-2

Published by Quadra Books
Victoria, BC, Canada
www.quadrabooks.com

For Alexander, Adam and Bill

Poems

Bones in the Deep Dirt

Poetry

There is a roundness I seek.
Most talk is flat,
a doormat
with the truth pressed out.
You step on it without noticing.
Wiping the dirt off.

Round talk
bumps against the body, soft,
touches through skin
it enters in with the breath.

I am sway, play:
secret sounds.
They resonate;
made for the first time.

I Will Take with Me

She will stand at the prow sniffing,
in my boat,
inside my shoes,
Prince, the Brittany Spaniel, as if she still lived.

When it is night on the water, I will make a song for the stars.
The story of my mother, stowed deep in a waterproof bag
I will take with me.
I will take with me

rolled scraps of paper, inside my shoes
my recorder—German rosewood, a soprano
with her hunter's nose and stub of tail.
My legs heavy and strong
I will take with me.

Forensic Anthropology

The work of the poet is archaeology, bones
deep dirt, diamonds, spades.

She shuffles the deck
flips each card to show colours, suits:
        red or black
        Heart or Club.

Stakes high
some want more, some less:
        an Ace
        a Queen
        a Joker.

Chandeliers dazzle at night.
She is a croupier, wears:
        white shirt
        black skirt
        red hat on a slant, perhaps with a bell.

She sits still, eyes only on shapes,
the flat surface of cards on a table.
Her hands move
sharp like surgery,

her fingers tapered long
her nails, a lawn filed clean
of human remains dug up
during hours of sunlight outside the casino.

The Body Waits for Me There

In the Servants' Quarters

The passage narrows as I climb and
sweat lands hot with salt
on my hand.

∞

Last night
I dreamed I was awake in this room
and saw a ghost.
There has been a killing.
The ghost sits in a chair that does not rock but
even though frozen in time, this ghost is never at rest.

In the dream in which I am awake
I tell her: "You have died."
I see hieroglyphs of blood
on walls which slope steep down
in this almost-attic room
in this house with stairs that wind up and
closets that turn corners
in the dark. Restlessness carries me while
everything is still. She does not rock in her chair.
It balances on its curve as if suspended.

"You are dead," I say, but I don't speak
of the killing or the meaning of the ancient text
smeared on the walls.
I carry her like a child,
as if the dim light can shine through this moment,
the image I have of her.
She weighs almost nothing, a waif, a chimera
and I carry her down the back stairs, three flights,
the staircase for servants, and I lay her down
in the root cellar of this house
and when I lay her down on the dirt
her apron crumbles to dust.

∞

I dreamt I was awake in this room
and I saw you. Almost transparent
you wait, perhaps sitting in a chair, or floating.
These are servants' quarters
up in the rafters of the brick house.
Something happened here a long time ago,
a long time ago you climbed up
the narrow servants' stairs to this room
to something, the dust a cold blanket,
two windows shut tight, velvet curtains.
And the house, the room, everything in it
have been waiting for this moment.
I am awake here in this dream
and I carry you in my arms

and somehow the light shines through your body
and this room
has been your hell under the eaves, stuck in this moment
for maybe one hundred years,
in your apron white but splotched
with spots of blood long dried.
The roof slopes down on either side and
though you seem to float, I cradle you
and walk down the stairs,
down to the earth at the bottom of this house,
this tomb that holds its history inside.

∞

I know I was awake once in this room,
the servants' quarters, up three flights, and
I must go up the back stairs to get here
so as not to be seen.

A Morning Poem

1.
The smell of burnt coffee. My roommate leaves
a pot on the stove for hours
the black slick a kind of homing device.
He was once in the union. Now he needs a place to stay.
2.
I imagine a room, a meeting of men,
hefty slabs. They've been sweating for some time now, sour
sitting around a bare table, stale armpits.
Buttocks shift in chairs
scrape the linoleum, jackets off and the air stiff
with stubble. Only cream scum remains in mugs
long drained of the java, coffee dregs left on the element
too long after midnight and no one thinks
to start afresh though their eyes sink into sockets
tongues lie thick in mouths, they utter monosyllables.
3.
With fresh brew at breakfast, I sit at a table
with police friends, now out of uniform,
tell them my coffee story.
Burnt coffee, they say, is the lesser of two evils.
When you're finally called to the house, sirens wail,
the body waits for you there,
maybe in a bed, maybe on the floor in the living room.
You cannot save it. It has been there for some time.
Go to the kitchen they tell me, burn coffee on a flame,
that darkness cuts through any other smell.

Script for the Inquest

In my dream
Marion Woodman falls asleep
while I speak, she nods off, pregnant virgin
in a white room. Her head leans
against the wall with no paintings.
While I speak.

Not in court today but here in this room.
I thought I had notes but all I have are crumpled bits
of paper, scraps with stickmen doing stretches scrawled there.
I thought I had something but
no, nothing. So I start without notes, with only diagrams
on death. This is my topic.

Five bodies found up the hill from my house:
grandparents, mother and the boy
named Christian. A hole cut into glass
so no alarm went off. The smell of gas
the chance of explosion, a fireball, a father's suicide.

I describe who died but the jury
has other ideas, other killings they want to bring to light
the light fades in the room and Marion is sleeping
in my dream,
too many people are dying while my jury members are lying
on mattresses strewn on the floor.

Isn't it time for a break? I have to take a pee
no, make a speech about who was really killed
up the street from my house. The police
discovered defensive wounds.
Running out, the light is running out. How to
sort this out? My jurors shout names
I do not know. They don't have their facts straight,
the fact of the matter. Shouting yes,
but the blond girl I see up front does not speak,
too young to sit on that mattress without sheets. Come,
revelations come from mattresses on the floor,
stickmen stretches, sketches in black ink on crumpled paper.

Scraps
people are hungry, it's time to eat instead of speak
and I move to join these laypeople on the pelvic floor.
We stretch
together in a line, our legs up the wall
with no paintings and a sleeping woman who is pregnant.
I have a crumpled bit of paper in my hand, some ink drawings.
This inquest. Bodies in a white room.

Ballroom Speech

She is a judge.
She is a woman in black robes, indigenous,
steps behind the lectern in this ballroom where we sit,
speaks of her university daughter who asks:
"What are you doing about it?"
 She means the missing and murdered women.

This ballroom where we sit
the audience filled with cops. There are no windows.
The men are not in uniform
and they don't carry guns in here
and no one dances the Foxtrot for long
long, short short or the Viennese Waltz, in a square
or is it a circle, the man leading.
He signals the woman with a hand pressed
into the small of her back.

And there is no graduation or gala to be seen
 in this ballroom. Even though chandeliers hang,
their million slivers glisten, globes of glass suspended.
The ice in our glasses, our eyes.

It is quiet in this ballroom full of men, their motto:
"To serve and protect."
A white cloth droops over the edge of the table
and we all listen to the woman,
the woman whose daughter asks: what now, or maybe why.

The room is a modern design,
the ceiling a clouded mirror
reflects light
and the woman stands, sings of her daughter
in this place where we sit around a table.
The men have lost their insignia, they have no rank.
Their large hands lie cupped in their laps.

The banquet is ending.
We wear formal attire
but there is no dancing.
The men move their thick fingers, flatten out
paper napkins, fold them
back in place alongside plates which carry
the cold remains of dinner.

The Usual

I watch those cops
poet cops, they like opera, maybe jazz, the blues
detectives who must set their jaws to face death or maybe
worse head-on.
I see them walk in a line.
They do not wear uniforms but dark suits, black
or blue, flattening their ties against the wind as they enter
the crime scene. The yellow warning tape not up yet.

I read their bodies as I follow,
the hold of the shoulders,
square front-on forward. No face
turns away to avoid demons. Steady steps,
march into a maelstrom: gravel scratches their soles as they
enter: a street, a sidewalk, a house,
a church, a temple, a cave. The soles of shoes,
the scrape of gravel.

something about rabbits

It all began at the university residence, or so it is said. A dorm room, a student alone, but he has two rabbits in a cage and we know where that leads. By the time you can tell them apart, the *'he'* and *'she'* have turned into *'they.'*

> When I arrive, I think I know about names, the birds and the bees. But in the amphitheatre, my first law professor says: *"You must ask yourself what the reasonable man on the Clapham Omnibus would do in the same circumstances."*

The boy lets the rabbit family loose in the field. The colony becomes a continent, plants and grasses stripped, million dollar turf an aperitif.

> In second year, I learn about guilty and innocent: *"We are advocates, not finders of truth."* This time we wear robes.

Outside moot court, I witness foreign students feeding rabbits they think are *wild*. At Easter they name newborns. Some are run over on their way to find food. At a fundraising dinner, university donors are given stuffed rabbits as gifts.

In my last year, I find myself lost in what they teach is
a *'legal fiction.'*

Under cover of darkness, the administration captures rabbits
old and young, cages and flies them to a rabbit sanctuary in
Texas.

At graduation I receive parting words: *"Watch what
judges **do**, not what they **say**."*

Soon the headline reads: *"Trouble in Texas: Canadian rabbits escape
from their compound, are shot with rifles, farmers angry over lost produce."*

At the university, new students arrive, drawn in by the story of
wild rabbits alive on campus. When truth dawns, these fresh
young minds dig up lawns in protest. They plant vegetables in
memory of the dead they never knew.

'De minimus no curat lex:' the law does not concern itself
with trifles.

Speechwriter in Magenta

The Justice Minister asks where I was born, hoping
it was somewhere else,
that I was part of the first generation
now landed on these winter shores,
his liberal country,
and did I just follow my husband
to this town,
and was I a journalist, because they can't write speeches,
and why did I work for the Justice Critic before,
that guy from the other party?

For work I wear
a magenta dress with African shapes.
The shopgirl shows me how
to tighten the belt.

On the job I learn:
the Justice Minister wants Arial font
all caps half way down the page
so he does not have to break
eye contact with the crowd.
He wants big words
under small lights on the dark podium:
justice
human rights.

A legal scholar,
he wants to be philosopher king.

When I write at the office,
I step into the maze of his mind,
see nothing but corners, letters
pressed onto moveable pieces
edges with no clues.
I tell myself—
This is just a job or
law school prepared me for this or
I can still walk in a straight line or
he doesn't know I know he's gay, just like The Justice Critic was,
that guy from the other party.
It's three dimensional Scrabble,
and some words never make it to the board:
power
pain.

Much later, I write remarks to be given in Cabbagetown.
The words lie flat on the page,
an array of letters, a cipher,
for the anniversary of the Stonewall Riots.
In the silence between lines:
massage parlours, police,
beautiful angry men beaten on black streets
the thud of batons, bones breaking.

My body ripens,
cracks open, produces a son.
I leave The Big Smoke, move west
back to earth, sky and sea. Motherland,
where my baby's cry floats like flotsam.
The slap of waves breaking on shore.

The magenta dress has come along
in my suitcase, then in the closet here for years,
now on my bed. I say goodbye
to the shopgirl who showed me this item
worn once by a runway model,
sold to me in the smallest size.

I smooth down the fabric, undo the belt
liberate
those African shapes that never made it to anyone's mouth.
My words rest on this page.
No podium, no reading light,
just a table, a pen
and a candle to see silhouettes.

Gettysburg: A Prose Poem

There is an American star and she dances with a baton and
there is marching music and she wears glitter and she may be
too old for this now and I wonder.

What if I lived in a country where we built huge statues of our
leaders and where we memorized some of their speeches like
the Gettysburg Address and put our hands on our hearts and
recited an oath together in a classroom every morning from
kindergarten on.

And what if one year we watched a TV show on the
anniversary of this speech and academics and scriptwriters
talked about it and a film had been made about it and this film
was nominated for an Oscar.

And what if the scriptwriter described the speech as a prose
poem.

And what if we knew that after he gave this speech, President
Lincoln got very sick with smallpox.

And what if one of the commentators on the TV show was a
black historian who knew all about the president's valet who
also happened to be black, dark black, which made it hard for
him to get into the White House even though the President
insisted.

And what if we heard that this black valet stayed by the President's side throughout his illness and that while the President got better after just three weeks, the valet died of it, caught smallpox from the President and died.

And what if at the end of this same TV show about the President's speech, we see the valet's gravestone with only his name on it and the word "citizen."

And what if we read in the paper the next day that the black soldiers who were killed at Gettysburg had to be buried in a different cemetery from the whites.

And what if we were all citizens of this country, a country where black men like Martin Luther King take words from the Gettysburg Address, stand in front of the huge statue of President Lincoln and weave his words into their own narrative.

And if I am told by a woman historian that Lincoln's wife pleaded with him not to go to Gettysburg in the first place because their young son was sick and might also be dying.

And if I find out the President goes anyway and the First Lady must stay behind. What would I say?

And if I am also told that the first person to hear the Gettysburg Address (in the President's hotel room the night before) is his valet.

What if I hear that when Lincoln gives his three minute
address to the people the next day, he speaks after someone
else who talked to the crowd for two hours. What if none of us
remember the name of the other speaker.

If I could share all these moments with my countrymen and
women, how would I feel? And what if I were then to say
certain words to them: independence, equality, a government
of the people, by the people, for the people.

And then what if I remembered a simple name and the word
'citizen' on a gravestone?

If I lived in a country such as this, would I look more like that
cheerleader twirling the polished object, that baton in my
fingers, hearing the fife and drum beat the march of many feet
following behind me in this place of monuments, idols,
invocations, oaths, a hand on the heart.

This glittering place where we still don't know if the
President's valet was born free.

Is he born free or does he still have to escape from the South
using the underground railway with the North Star, that speck
in the sky, as his compass.

No Woman Should

A woman should not speak her wishes out loud
and if she does, she must knock twice on the wood table,
keep the demons out.

Find a penny pick it up,
find another one get bad luck.
Salt in the sugar bowl.

And God help us if you cut that undercooked potato
with your knife, which should never be passed
over to your husband
with the blade facing out.

And no woman should ever crush the spider in her bed
even though it may creep in the crease
keep her up all night.

Going to the Ghost World

Musical Range

Descant, soprano
alto, contralto
tenor, bass.
Crampons like claws
bound to the bottom of boots.
Climber's descent, helmet on head
axe in hand
down snow slopes
over ice fields

to deep parts.
Low tones. Long shadow, black line.
Crack in the clef, a crevice cold. Ice picks
rock. The pitch, a cliff fall,
force of gravity.

Bassoon, baritone, bass clarinet
string bass. These players sit in the back.
Piano: played with only the left hand,
lower register.

Octaves drop. Black keys depressed
dark hole, orchestra pit. Vast.
Abyss.

No dancing.
Here is heavy: no tapping feet no tune.
Here there is no light.

Many don't care to listen.
Their ear is for melody.
They climb high ranges, peaks,
thin air,
perhaps a mask to breathe.
They have a head for heights.

Dizzy dog whistles,
piccolos, flutes
first violins: the concert masters.
People clap when they enter, musicians all stand
the baton, a wand held high
in the hand of a man, he wears a tuxedo, bow tie.

Still,
there has to be a bottom somewhere,
even in music.

Before I Die

I want to read every book in my shelf
written in Gothic script by
authors unknown, inscribed to
a young German woman who laughs.
I have seen her in pictures, she carries my name.

In my yard I want to
sit on the blue stone,
wait while it warms me.
I want to see the pregnant raccoon
enter the hollow to give birth inside
the Garry Oak trunk tangled in
dead English Ivy.

Before I die
I want to swing out into
the river near a place called Thrums, on a twisted rope,
let go and fall into the current floating
with no thought of shore.

I Will Ask My Mother about It Today

1.
There is a photo of me,
a tough-looking toddler but
not in this shot.

I sit pudgy, loose.
In the arch of my arm
I cradle my baby,

the white doll.
The crown of her head faded brown,
rough with ridges.
Plastic body, plasticized hair.

Meticulous, I tip
droplets of water into my doll's eyes
with the ritual spoon.
It's silver and I believe in her.

I tip water
into her eyes painted open,
look to see what happens
to the tears I have given her, tears I have dropped.

My baby and I sit solid
on the cushion of my mother's thighs.
A mother who smiles
in this photo.

2.
She has come back from her journey
across the hospital hall.
My mother went to see her friend
whose body lies with
the empty eyes.

My mother, shuffled across
in her hospital gowns, sky blue
one worn backwards, a cape
to cover the hump of her back.

"A dead body," I ask,
"when was the last time
you saw the dead?"
She won't go too far back in her mind
to the time of corpses frozen like boards.

3.
On the wall hangs
another photo, this one framed,
the glass broken, jagged in two places.

"Jack" she says, "my second husband, the Englishman."
He smiles in the picture,
eyes crinkled behind steel frames.
"I never touched his body,
could not carry the urn of ashes.
He is closer, now," she adds.

Flame

1.

I sit before the hearth
watch the fire.
Shadows stretch the room.
One flame left, flutters as if a candle.
Black logs still hot
glow orange inside.
The rustle, the shift of a tree limb breaking up.
Ash drops through bars of the grate.
This fire, set inside an archway of stone, a gate.

2.

Her body will be framed, encased before it burns.
I imagine trees along the shore.
The land where she grew up was flat, the river broad and fast.
My mother has come far
in her new land of mountains.

3.

I ride in the current of an SUV
on a road through Fraserview Cemetery.
My brother drives.
A speed limit sign passes us,
we stick to it, still somehow seeming to speed
towards the chapel. I see the chimney.

4.

I am the last woman standing.
I came late to the wake and wailed.
I helped with clothes to be worn in the coffin.
A rose coloured cardigan,
my mother's best colour, the blush in her cheeks.
The question of shoes.

I have imagined this.
The casket will be open, the eyes closed.
I will caress the cold cheek.
I will go in alone.

Dark wood will frame the body
like a hollowed out tree trunk
an ancient water craft ready for flame.
I go in alone.

Aubade

Finding My Father's Voice

Dawn lies between us
a gift of glacier water painful to drink.
I tip ice pellets into the side of your mouth
lips now parched, a desert.

Words have passed here and been lost
many sharp breaths taken in
held in my belly, braced.

Somehow my silence grew in another garden
my seed carried there
on another animal's body, caught on a branch
then dropped.

Now is the time of the grey light, the hardening off,
the deadfall. Men come in uniform
pick up branches scattered by the wind.

To get here I traveled through snow,
driving in ruts. For years I carried your guitar
without its case. At home I played the baby grand.

Now there is glacier water in your mouth.
My son cradles your guitar, sings at your side.
His voice breaks,
your body on the bed, stiff limbs
waiting to dance.

Lineage

After Patrick Lane's Poem 'Family'

My father is an axe swung high overhead,
his steel edge
just catches that glint of sun out back.
His blade whistles down through space,
his handle gripped by some unseen executioner.

My mother is a pair of walking boots
grabbed and put on two feet, quick
when the soldiers come to the house,
just before the long forced march
into winter.

Now, no one is home.

I am the gate to the garden.
My latch is unlocked, my hinges creak
open shut, open shut,
the force of an oncoming storm.

Schumi's Turn

The clock strikes in my Aunt Hedwig's house in Bonn
Gertrude and I drink dark afternoon coffee, eat apricot torte.
My aunt serves and Gertrude raises her cup from its saucer,
tells me about my mother at school:

This nun would line us up, our palms open
as if to receive the communion wafer, then
whack us one by one with a stick.
We all pulled our hands back
when she stood before us, that black spectre,
it was just before the war.

Schumi's turn comes, your mother,
she is quick, she runs from the lineup
here there everywhere
in and out of rows all around the classroom
knocks over desks as she turns

the nun must give chase, her dark habit askew
your mother's blond curls fly.
The rest of us stay in line
purse our lips, hold our breath to bursting
bubbles of laughter escape our throats
to join Schumi in flight.

Gertrude puts her coffee cup down on the saucer
she still holds,
that porcelain sound in this living room now.
My aunt shakes her head, smiles,
offers more torte.

A late sun bounces back from the hall mirror
I squint as rays hit my face
apricots sweet on my tongue.

Insignia

Aryan
the teacher says it
and writes the word with chalk on a blackboard.
Her students sit at desks
eyes open but blank.
They must be taught.

"What does an Aryan girl look like?"
they ask. The teacher walks to my mother's desk
"Ursula, please stand up."

My mother is tall, a blonde,
clear blue eyes look ahead.
She is a high jumper, long jumper, swimmer,
a winner of badges and ribbons. Prowess,
proud to stand at attention, a specimen
in a schoolroom with other children
and nuns who teach.

I see her,
already in uniform:
pleated skirt, tailored jacket, wool stockings,
leather shoes laced tight
to feet that want to run, to leap high
wide over any closed gate.

Prowess.
It may have saved her
in the end,
in the hunger times when she was conscripted
to work on the assembly line in a factory that made bombs.

I think I see her now in a classroom
still standing in this picture she has given me
an emblem without a frame,
a gift of honour
and shame.

Questions I Always Wanted to Ask My Mother

How did you swing it? After the war.
How did you break free,
the train so full that no handholds were left.
You had to belt yourself onto the last car, onto the railing,
that balcony off the end of the German caboose rumbling off
and away,
that grey that I see in pictures.
There is no photo of this. You lean back,
the dark smoke, the wind, the wave of your hair, long then.
How did you do this?
The arch of your back. The iron of the last car leaving,
the track ahead,
the swell of your abdomen ripe with child.

Going to Germany

It's not only boats that cross water.
Travelling morse code messages
make a foreign sound:
tapping, dots and dashes
abstract on the page.

Going back with a new suitcase,
hard red.
Arriving with no key.
A father searches through his old collection
to find one that fits.

Leaving the motherland,
two toddlers tied together
with rope on the decks of the winter Atlantic
sick with loss and the tossing.

Then a father's death.
Trying to return.
Papers invalid.
Crying before a man in uniform.
A sudden softening, the stamp of approval
and the movement towards something.

Now a son leaves home.
He must cross a huge new continent to go back,
first by train.
The holding at the station, the dark eyes,
the damp faces left behind.
Empty shoes with loose laces,
the unknown return.

The visit of a sister,
her death by water.
The gravestone sent over.
The search for remains.

Bodies lost
and at least two languages
once tied down to place.
The entry codes sometimes forgotten.
Numbers and buttons on a tiny key pad.
The overseas telephone voice gets fainter.
The receiver no longer holds the sound.

Gisela Renate

In this poem I am not named Gisela.
In grade one, I do not take chalk from Miss Estey's hand
at Shaughnessy Elementary,
write each letter, upper case bold on the blackboard.
I do not think: if my name is written right
they will understand.

Not being Gisela, I do not know
that Craig Campbell and John Stark call me Gizzard.
I don't remember them
their simple names with no history.
I don't witness
the stumble, the stutter of tongues as people say Geesla.
I do not wait for questions:
What a pretty name!
What nationality are you?

Without Gisela, I do not have my secret narrative:
born during June flood waters, near the river
on the front seat of our Meteor in the Monashee Mountains.
Yes, born in a car, the meteor momentarily stopped here
mid-flight.

Not being Gisela,
I do not hear when my father says:
learn Latin, the root of rational language.
Nor do I hear when he tells me about
Renate, my middle name,
that Gisela Renate means Gisela reborn.

When I graduate from law school,
my father Helmut doesn't perform the song
he once sang with my German aunt during Fasching,
carnival-time in the Rhineland,
before the war when they were young, still dancing.
This song, for Gisela, the aunt I was named after,
my mother's little sister.

Tante Gisela,
who came for a short visit after the war,
drowned, swept over the falls in the Shuswap River,
her grave dug in Kelowna.
Gisela, her headstone sent over from Europe
to North America, that desert, bare earth and sky
no gothic arch, no bell tower, no ancient bell to ring.

And my mother Ursula,
with no memory of the name, the river,
does not walk into the graveyard with a shovel, dig the dirt
to move the marker, to always carry it with her:
the headstone of her German sister
now dead in the Okanagan.

Since my name is not Gisela,
my mother does not give me her sister's gravestone
one day in Victoria, a place named after an English queen,
this dead weight carried from desert to coast,
this marker carved in Rheinland-Pfalz. Dark wood cut
into the shape of a steeple, sent over in a plane.

In this poem I am Renate.
I see photos of my mother Ursula, her sister Gisela,
she who escaped from the Shuswap River,
later also emigrated to Canada.
I look at the two women now, silhouettes in black and white.
 They face each other; laugh, well into the light.

Memory, Angel

Apples are ready.
Now there is no wind, no rain.
Against the wall, stucco and branches.
My parents are dead.
I separate one fruit from another,
hold them round, sweet, cold, cupped in my palm.

Across the water I can see my sister in her kitchen
cut the tart into four equal parts,
four siblings. Raisins drop
from the edge of her knife.

Paring Knife

Rusted but still deadly.
Sharp, short, discoloured, curved blade like a hook.
Imprint of the knife makers' logo:
two stick figures, silhouette twins locked frozen, arm in arm,
planted on the knife's edge.
Henckels Zwillinge.

This kitchen gift carried by my mother from somewhere.
Every item a harsh history.

Her hands grip green beans, the ends sliced,
blade stops short of her thumb.

I reach for it now, her agility,
to peel the peach. The handle gets lost in my hands,
my hold not firm enough, not fine enough.
Two figures. Paring fruit. *Get a grip.*
Never any blood in my mother's kitchen.

Headcheese

I come home from school to an empty kitchen,
pot on the stove, a stockpot
tall, narrow and lidless, stainless steel,
and rising over the rim I glimpse
a pig's snout, grey colour of meat not quite cooked.

My mother is nowhere I can see,
but every bit of that head,
the brain of the pig will be used.

They say pigs are smart—headcheese.
Bits of meat suspended in gelatin.

She liked cow's tongue too and blood sausage,
all the animal elements.

Steam fills the room
a gamey smell.

Silent Letters

*One wonderful thing about German spelling is that you basically spell how
you hear the word. There are not many exceptions.*
Ingrid Bauer, German Language Expert.

Lodz: slush on ground, graves,
bare branches. My son has sent pictures
ditches dug in 1941,
shroud of grass grows in the pit,
a depression that's left.

My son sends pictures.
I see his photo of the plaque,
a memorial, a literal call: Denkmal—
think now it says. Think!

Words are written in two languages, one
I still speak.
Letters small, pressed deep into black stone
on my screen that flickers.
I must blow the image up
to read it
in Polish and German.

Here it is aloud in English:

In this graveyard
over 700 Roma and Sinti lie buried.
They died
of hunger, sickness, exhaustion
in the Litzmannstadt Ghetto. Deported
from Burgenland by Nazis, 1941.
The remaining 1300,
the ones that survived,
were deported
to a concentration camp in Kalmhof
and murdered
in 1942.

In German it can be worse,
a language where every letter makes a sound.
Words can be worse,
like weapons, wounds,
stretchers that carry the dead: *Entkräftung, Erkrankung,*
Ermordung
exhaustion, disease, murder.

English may be my home language,
mother tongue of vowels,
silent spots, pools within words, lacunae. Learning to spell.
I write letters down. They sometimes lie mute:
foreigner, receive.
Consciousness.

Here
we don't say silent letters
don't cry out, make the voice carry.

Where are the sounds
when I need them, when I read the plaque from Poland,
my fingers on a keyboard, the digital image, dark,
sent by my son

from Lodz. He stays in a place I remember
where spring is slow to start,
where old men make vodka in basements.
Vodka like water, words,
a homemade drink of ice
that burns the throat.

The Frankfurt School

Long bones, the long train snakes
its way to Frankfurt, to find Adorno, Marcuse.

The long bones of the young man among many
on the train today to join the protest, someone
has thrown themselves onto the track he rides.
It could be any day.

The young man waits on the train.
He sits with other students who speak a dialect
he must lean in to learn.
The tracks must be cleansed, the driver unhinged
from his seat, his harness unbuckled.
He just had time
to look into the eyes of the jumper beforehand,
it was too late.

In Frankfurt, train doors open
the long line of protesters
a current of thousands.
Banks line the street.
The students step forward with placards, letters held high
 and voices that cry with the new language learned on the train.

It could be any day.
Thousands snake
into narrow streams, streets, far below
an economic summit, talk in steel towers.
Outside young bodies glisten, their voices ripple,
blocked before a line of police
truncheons, masks, many wounded,
faces cry tears from the gas,
but apart from the train jumper, no one is killed
on this day.

The young man has studied philosophy,
being and nothingness.
His own river rises brown over its banks
roots torn away. The Frankfurt School.
Boats once tethered to a shoreline that now disappears.

The Burgundy Effect

She traces her finger along the line of my map
shows me a different route down.
Born in Stuttgart 1945, she knows the terrain.
We stand on Feldberg, highest peak on the
edge of the Black Forest.

Hills here topped with trees, valley floor a marsh.
Vines grow along a strip on southern slopes.
The trees like guardians, stop frost that kills, catch wind
so grapes can ripen. The Burgundy Effect,
Spätburgunder, a red wine rare in these parts.

She tells me she wrote a newspaper
column about food and drink, hikes alone.
We eat chocolate.
She won't speak about the war, what her parents did
or did not do.
Worse in cities, where even winter potatoes were scarce.

She takes me to the Jewish graveyard,
a wooden gate back against the north side
letters in Hebrew carved into stone. Moss.
We are caught in a thunder shower,
drenched as we stare into grey and green
this place left alone, a dark slope.

Todtnauberg a village on my map, not far:
Heidegger's Hut, Celan's poem. The two met there,
walked in the woods, 1967.
Martin impressed with Paul's knowledge of plants.
A tincture of Arnica. A salve of Eyebright.
Botany was what they could share.

My Stuttgart friend and I hike overseas now
bring wine to the desert.
We see markers, cairns for the dead.
We stop, kneel down into dust, saying the names.

My Mother Wove Me a Blanket

Clumps of uncarded wool
cupped in my hands.
Oily, sticky to touch,
shorn from sheep trotting together,
through green ravines, rivers of mist.
Animal breath warms the damp day.

Our spinning wheel
a redwood sculpture
amidst flotsam in the family den.
Pump the pedal, see how fast the wheel can spin.
The whir and thump, forbidden pleasure.

Her hands hear the call:
fleece to wool, spun on the wheel,
wool to cloth, woven on the loom.
Something for cover, disguise.

I wear that blanket,
draped heavy as a shield,
other days it's a pelt
almost alive.

Heart Mechanic

Heart Mechanic

In my house something
is always broken, on the verge.
Roof shingles warped, gutters glutted. Even
the door handle stuck. I take up
hammer and nails, pick paint colours for cover.
Windows are dirty.
I speak the monosyllabic talk
of unskilled day labour.

But you, the heart mechanic just
around the curve of my street, outside
just where I can't see you.
But there are signs. Branches
clipped back, the touch of air, oil on a gate hinge.

Come in with your special tools,
take the hammer from my hand,
melt down those nails. If necessary
draw blood. See my tear ducts open,
feel the flow of salt water
over my ancient wound.

Gift of the Gull

1.
Summer, on Passage Island,
my sister and I find a gull's nest.

We think the parents have left,
looking for food,
leaving their young unprotected.

But every time we reach out to touch the speckled eggs,
as if it were Easter Sunday,
globs and goops of fishy shit rains down,
on our hair, our bare necks.

2.
Spring, James Bay.
I call my mother.
Her highrise looks over the sea.
Her voice message includes a garbled sound: *Kaakkaakkaak.*
The gull voice,
the voice they use with their own kind,
in close quarters where they are safe.

The roof of the highrise is flat
home to a colony built by birds.
From daybreak to dark,
my mother, embedded in a nest of seagull sound.

3.
Winter gale, Ross Bay,
power lines dangle, pop, tree branches drop.
Waves thrash, hurtle over pavement
into the graveyard, seaside rest
for sailors killed by storms, the earth of graves
stirred up. Gulls dip and
tip their wings into wind, soar along the line
between water and land,
their high call, that scree
reserved for big places.

4.
A Fall workshop, Vancouver: *The Mastery of Self Expression.*
Instructions: make only animal sounds.
I am a gull, I don't sing or warble in a treetop.

No, I make raw sounds of the shore,
hurt my chest, throat, head.
I do not use my tongue, my brain.

After this exercise
my feedback form says:
I don't know what kind of animal you were trying to be
but the sounds you made were obscene.
Like shit
they have no place inside a building.

The Beginning of White

Midsummer.
My son loads hay bales into the loft
leather gloves loose on thin fingers
hard to grip.
A black lab with eight nipples, pregnant with nine puppies,
content to squat slantwise, pee in the dust.
I speak to the farm woman.
The mare whinnies,
bangs her hooves against the gate.

I speak to the woman,
with black stubble above her lips and
rimless glasses, eyes blue.

I tell her of the chicken deaths
at the other farm I knew.
The mystery of these creatures. They dropped dead
with no outward mark. Autopsies performed.
Those fast beating hearts had stopped short from fear—simply
the sight of something killed them.

Today we talk of two Garry Oaks that blew down last winter.
By the barn my son sits atop towering hay bales,
looks back at us from the moving truck.

On the limb of a living oak
a bird of prey, a hunchback, sits,
not startled by our stance,
two women, one already a crone.
What is this bird? A vulture?

But only the young stay so close. This eagle,
black body cloaked, face shadowed,
swivels his head around
his face turned back to see us.

Eyes sharp, yellow talons grip the limb.
No movement.
But in time he opens his wings for that first flight.
We see the underside, juvenile speckles,
the beginning of white.

Superwoman

If I played the drums
I would be at the root of things.
My arms muscled and bared with jungle tattoos.
I would swing dark dreadlocks, swear in a screaming voice
pitched high. Part of the pulse.

If I sang solo before a packed house
a cappella, my eyes would hold yours.
We would inhabit mansions of sound.
We would vibrate like a single human instrument
played by a demigod, a demon.

If I danced around the bushfire
at midnight, dressed in rags,
I would feel flame lick my limbs and yours,
burnt black to the bone.

I will bare my chest.
I will let you see the veiled peaks and valleys.
I will take your hand and hold it on my scar
in the shape of a cross.
The umbilicus is deep in my belly.
The place of union and of loss.

Spa Girl

She loves steam—indeed
liquids in any form, floating, cascading.

Roman pillars, lotions, notions, oils, archways
a slick left behind in the mineral pool,
sandals left at the door.

On the neck, Lavender oil from the purple plant,
on the shoulders, Balm of Gilead
from bark of the Cottonwood Tree.

Her bare skin stroked sleek. Spa girl sips and
her body, weightless, floats.

The Erratic

Cold, hard, I stand.
Eternity. Nothing moves.

But from inside and beyond, a new age:
a wrenching.
A grip, a grind.
Ice tears away, the muscle rips cold.
Layers come apart. Tendons scream.
The bones, the brokenness begins.

Parts of myself in retreat now,
I can see
there is no blood
only water that once was ice,
so clear.

Along the path,
solids scrape solids,
scars etched forever into stone.

Turning Fifty with a Friend

There was no family car available
so we rented.

It was hot
so we got an SUV with air conditioning.

Just the two of us
in a silver icicle truck
over the Coquihalla Pass.

When we got to our cabin it was hotter than our bodies.
so we drove the icicle truck to the lake.

Apart from the beach, we spent most days naked inside.
Like your time in the tropics, you said
and I followed suit. Even the nights were hot.

Friends forgot us.
Kids and husbands fended for themselves

as we lay on our separate beds, lay
on our sides, talking across the narrow space in between.

Soon, even the trip to the corner store for food
seemed perilous, a flight to the red planet.
Something beyond our dreams,
that distant planet outside with rocks, no water and
the risk of alien encounters.

Blowdrying My Hair in Public

Getting out of the change room shower I see
a device which looks like the clamps they use
for electroshock therapy.
It's costly to straighten the hair.
When the young woman plugs it in,
the fire alarm light goes on,
flashing red but with no alarm.

In the designated room for blowdryers
another woman stands tall in mauve underwear,
almost a salute.

In the playpen a naked mother dresses her baby. Lickety split.
A pregnant woman wants to hold him.

I've never done this in public before
smoothing split ends with my cylindrical brush, the bristles.
Old woman with a knee brace sits on a bench among towels.

Floor grout rises up, slime between my toes.
Coins click in lockers. My skin glows,
a purple tone under fluorescent lights.
Hair products rest on a ledge,
mirrors.

Almost There:
A Walk to the Beach on the Cote D'Azur

Behind the stone wall on the walk
a guard dog snarls, protects
the empty greenhouse.

∞

Outside: Oleander, Lavender, Bougainvillea, Agave
Eucalyptus, Cyprus, Hibiscus
Portulaca, Yucca the size of a small car
Cicadas call. Maybe a night ferry to Corsica
or a walk to the beach at Carqueiranne.

La Mediterranee.
Two lifeguards stand watch
under a blue parasol.
A young man wears a purple wig,
fights, and is thrown into the water by friends.
A raft floats with no ladder.
A man sweats in running shoes,
hand-delivers a bouquet to certain sunbathers.
A beach waiter holds up a lobster
turned deep red on the grill
Bouillabaisse for later.

A young woman's tongue
licks drips of chestnut ice cream from a cone
before it disappears.
Restaurant tables rest on hot sand
each table top numbered with a stone from the sea.
Champagne swallowed but no real food,
quick gulps from narrow glasses.

Paunchy men clumped tight in talk before a beach bar.
Woman on a blanket, asleep on her back,
mouth open.

∞

Very few bodies here
swim in the water.
On a sign you can see the faint word written:
Xanadu.

Things I Like about the Moon

Picasso

Between you and me it's glass.
I can see a row of wild faces
perched over your shoulder, the demons
and the empty vessels.

I can see a row of wild faces.
They drop sharp shadows against the stone wall at your back
and the empty vessels.
Between us is glass.

They drop sharp shadows against the stone wall at your back.
Between us you have drawn a devil.
Between us is glass,
horns and hooks, claws that scrape.

Between us you have drawn a devil.
The stylus in your hand,
horns and hooks, claws that scrape.
The stylus clutched between dirty nails of thumb and index
finger, pointing.

The stylus in your hand.
Perched over your shoulder, the demons.
The stylus clutched between dirty nails of thumb and index
finger, pointing.
Between you and me it's glass.

Poem for the Last Day

In my garden an owl sits high
in the oak, his body is bark,
his branch a throne. As if rooted there for centuries unseen
before words were invented, a monarch of the tree
his head turned away from me
to that murder of crows,
vassals hop and caw
jump from twig to twig sideways
up and down with the occasional flap
to save themselves from dropping black,
in the face of his gaze, a laser that burns away
wounds and also kills.
The head that swivels, the gaze that meets my eyes.

Galiano on the Rocks

*The maenads were Dionysus' followers and enthusiastic participants in
wine-filled orgies. In the height of their ecstasy the maenads could tear
apart young animals destined for sacrifice.*

Mermaids could have been invented here,
breasts on hot rocks facing west
in a place named for a Spanish sailor
known as Dionisio.
Dionisio Galiano. Hundreds of years ago. Here.
Eating grapes with his female followers,
mermaids or is it maenads? Those crazed killers who eat
the flesh of their mates after the orgy.
A starfish impaled on a stake nearby
keeps the wasps away.

Cave Women

We run to a cave, wounds are
deep in the mountain and we lick them
till the blood runs clear from our tongues. At the cave mouth

we drop our fur coverings, our calluses
from carrying clubs
      our bodies hardened like the men who march,
      the many men on open prairie, their limbs swinging
      like spears.

Inside our dark hollow we smear the cave wall
with hand prints of ash, blood, we follow bloodlines, bone
traces in stone.

Before they give birth, some dogs still dig
a deep den. Before they give birth, these bitches,
if they are still wild enough.

Reindeer with Fur

You knead the dough for feather buns.
I cut chocolate cake I made for my son's birthday.

You wear the crucifix I bought at the Vatican.
I ask: *did Cliff have to convert?*

You have flour dust on your black shirt.
My hands are sticky.

I talk about knitting lessons.
You ask: *did Ursula make that wool vest you're wearing?*

To sleep, you wear an oxygen mask.
I shake my bottle of pills.

You make porridge.
I buy coffee for your new machine: The Pixie

Christmas is coming.

You light the fire.
I carry the bag that once held my mother's ashes.

Dignity it says on the side.

You phone the Cenacle Sisters about spiritual direction.
I walk past the Catholic Hospital I used to visit.

I give you socks with reindeer.
You give me boots with fur.

I stand on the hilltop where we first met.
With your daughter, you share the dark cake I brought.

Your house stands on the street where my mother died.
My house stands on the street where you were born.

In your hallway, a table with photos of children
and a father who is dead.
In my sunroom a basket of stones.

Outside, it snows.

Things I Like About the Moon

It holds the sun's light
but does not demand.

It changes shape
while remaining constant.

You can look it in the eye
but like sadness or sex, it often dances behind a veil of clouds.

Without fanfare
it pulls the tides of seven seas.

Its skin is scarred, changes colours.
Before rain, it wears a copper halo.

When it does something exceptional
we call it blue.

Happy is over the moon.
It makes shadows only some of the time.

Smooth round or crescent sharp,
its gender is not fixed.

When it brims full with strong juice,
sane people lie pinned in bed, awake, with their blinds closed.

Crazy people break windows, climb down knotted sheets,
escape from buildings barefoot.

Dogs jump onto the tops of empty picnic tables
to be closer and howl.

Cats on fence rails mate and yowl.
In the back garden night flowers bloom.

And on the beach, the dark blanket of water is pulled
low down to the pubic rock.

And a million tiny water creatures
find themselves suddenly on land.

Gisela Ruebsaat writes poetry as a way of understanding voice, family, work and life. Her poems have been included in anthologies from Quadra Books and LEAF Press. She has published, together with Heather McLeod, several scholarly articles about poetic voice and writing as personal inquiry. **Heart Mechanic** is her debut collection.

www.ingramcontent.com/pod-product-compliance
Lightning Source LLC
Chambersburg PA
CBHW031400060726
47590CB00007B/2869